METALLICA

Jon Hotten

ORION

AN ORION PAPERBACK

This is a Carlton Book

First published in Great Britain in 1993 by Orion Books Ltd,
Orion House, 5 Upper St Martin's Lane, London WC2H 9EA

Text and design copyright © 1993 Carlton Books Limited
CD Guide format copyright © 1993 Carlton Books Limited

A CIP catalogue record for this book is available from the British Library.

ISBN 1 85797 569 3

Edited, designed and typeset by Haldane Mason
Printed in Italy

THE AUTHOR
Jon Hotten
Jon Hotten is a rock journalist and author. He is a regular contributor to numerous rock
magazines.

Contents

Introduction

When you walk into a Metallica gig the first thing you smell is sweat and the first thing you see is frenzy. The first—and the only—thing you hear is the cause of all that sweat, all that frenzy. It's a gut-wrenching, heated, pounding, visceral wall of sound that began in a Los Angeles garage and now thunders in 11 million homes courtesy of the *Metallica* album.

Metallica have taken a deal of flak for that sound, because they made it grow up from blistering, speed-freak roots to a giant, riff-led aural spectacle that fills up stadiums. That is an injustice, for Metallica's achievement in taking thrash metal out of the ghetto and into mainstream acceptance is a huge one. Theirs is extreme music, and they've defied logic and commercial boundaries in selling over 20 million albums of chart-unfriendly, radio-bruising heavy metal. There are bands that owe their good living to Metallica.

Metallica are the unlikeliest of superstars, a band born in the image of the New Wave of British Heavy Metal (NWOBHM) of the late Seventies and early Eighties, a movement that spawned a motley collection of stars, stalwarts and uglies—the likes of Def Leppard, Iron Maiden, Saxon, Angel Witch,

Samson, Diamond Head and Venom. The latter two—riff kings Diamond Head from the British West Midlands and the ground-breakingly extreme Venom, from the north-east of the country—were considerable influences. Now Metallica have outgrown them all—even Def Leppard, whose diamond-hard radio grooves handed the Yorkshiremen massive success.

Given a strong root to draw on, Metallica spearheaded the thrash metal explosion that centred on San Francisco's Bay Area and produced Exodus, Megadeth and Possessed. As their fledgling career exploded, Metallica followed a textbook career path—hot demo, independent record deal, major management, major record deal, huge touring schedule, massive-selling LPs!

But if things were that simple, every Joe Blow and his dog would be a megastar. Metallica cut it because at their core is the ability to play great, innovative music and the integrity not to compromise that ability.

In their triumph, there has been tragedy, too. Much-loved bassist Cliff Burton perished in a tourbus crash just as the band were about to break. Metallica grieved and then conquered. This is what happened.

CHAPTER ONE

A Metal Revolution

Lars Ulrich was an unlikely kid to start a heavy metal revolution. First, he was from Denmark, a country not noted for its contribution to grease, studs and rock 'n' roll madness. Second, he was not rock god material—he was more a skinny, zitty lad with a headful of wild hair and the one-eyed approach to music of the superfan.

Bizarrely, it was a talent for tennis that started the whole grinding, supercharged, dollar-spinning Metallica engine running.

Ulrich's father, Torben, enjoyed a globe-trotting spell as a tennis pro, and his son displayed similar talent, gaining a Top 10 junior ranking in

Lars Ulrich—an unlikely man to start a heavy metal revolution!

Denmark. But when Ulrich was sent to Florida to expand his on-court skills, he ran slap bang up against his destiny in a local record shop instead.

The owner fed him *Survivors*, a new album by Samson, a young British band. The music was raw, untutored metal—not the muso-head rock of Seventies giants Deep Purple or Led Zeppelin, but the punk-tinged garage metal of keen brains and fumbling fingers. Workmanlike, sure, but fired by true belief—and it was the genesis of the New Wave of British Heavy Metal (NWOBHM), a clumsy yet lovable acronym for the first post-punk metal that was coined by a youthful British journalist called Geoff Barton.

Ulrich, who'd been hooked on heavy rock since making a spectacularly early concert-going début by checking out the aforementioned Deep Purple at the age of nine, had his metallic mind blown. To understand why, it's necessary to check out what young ears had been subjected to just before the NWOBHM took clammy hold and roasted off new ears.

The birth of the NWOBHM

The summer of 1976 saw England and Europe pinned down by punk. Suddenly kids everywhere decided that a degree in music wasn't a pre-requisite for forming a rock 'n' roll band. Copping this anti-social backlash right in the pay-packet were the dinosaurs of bloated Seventies rock—Deep Purple, Genesis, Yes, ELP, Led Zeppelin *et al.* When the punk hurricane blew out, a slightly younger generation—Thin Lizzy, Judas Priest, AC/DC—made chart inroads, delighting in the renewed

NWOBHM donuts Samson's redeeming feature was that they had Bruce Dickinson (then Bruce Bruce) as their lead singer. He later fronted Iron Maiden to glory.

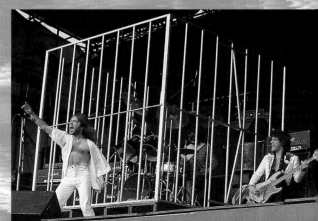

Def Leppard: one of the NWOBHM bands to hit superstar status—despite the dodgy dress sense!

popularity of aggressive music. Then the NWOBHM took the punk ethic and added the traditional metal elements of dramatic imagery and shocking stage-shows to create a vibrant new scene.

America's metal scene

America, as usual, lagged behind. When the Ulrich family relocated to the US in 1980, settling in Huntingdon Beach, California—initially to aid Lars's tennis career—the airwaves were awash with soft rock. Journey, Foreigner, Styx and REO Speed-wagon—the ultimate antithesis of punk—ruled. The LA scene that would later dominate was embryonic. Bands like Mötley Crüe, Ratt, Dio and Armoured Saint were taking their first tentative steps.

But from America, Ulrich was able to keep pace with the NWOBHM, although the phenomenon was alien to the West Coast. The British scene was already sizzling when Motorhead—the grizzly great uncles of the NWOBHM, led by legendary warthog Lemmy—smashed to the top of the album charts with their landmark (and deafening) live record, *No Sleep Til Hammersmith*, in 1981.

Thus inspired, the NWOBHM exploded. Ulrich got an earful of Saxon via their seminal *Wheels Of Steel* LP, and kept in touch with the scene via the weekly paper *Sounds*. Def Leppard cut their *Getcha Rocks Off* EP, Praying Mantis, Angel Witch and Tygers Of Pan Tang perpetuated the movement; Iron Maiden, pulled together in the heart of London's working-class East End, released *The Soundhouse Tapes* and promptly signed the major deal with EMI that set them on their way to superstardom, while Bruce Dickinson, the man who would eventually front them to glory, cut his teeth with the aforementioned fellow-strugglers Samson.

Venomous influence

Then came Venom, a savage and massively influential trio from northeast England who played music more extreme than any heard before. Long before the term "thrash

Iron Maiden with the legendary Eddie the Ed centre-stage.

metal" was coined, Venom clouted out what they called "black metal", a blistering carnival of speedy riffage and almost unintelligible vocals imbued with imagery of devils, hell and mayhem.

Initially regarded as joke, Venom were to bring influence to bear on the Bay Area thrash scene of which Metallica would become such an integral part.

Enter Diamond Head

But Ulrich's—and Metallica's—greatest inspiration came powering out of Stourbridge, a provincial town in central England. Diamond Head—fuelled by Brian Tatler's immense, Zeppelin- and Sabbath-tinged riffing and Sean Harris's Robert Plant-like range and strutting stage presence—were a band who didn't fulfil their massive potential first time around, but none the less provided a tantalizing glimpse of greatness.

Ulrich grabbed an earful of their 1980 single 'Helpless'/'Shoot Out The Lights'. He began writing to the band regularly, and then, in the summer of 1981, flew to the UK to follow Diamond Head's British tour.

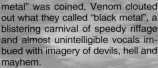

The British black metal gods Venom gave Metallica an early break via the Seven Dates of Hell tour.

After using his now-legendary gift of the gab to charm his way into meeting the band, Ulrich soon found himself as first Sean Harris's houseguest, then Brian Tatler's.

He devoured every bit of information Diamond Head could give him, both on themselves and the rest of the NWOBHM, and cemented a friendship with the band that continues today. Tatler also recalls Ulrich spending large wads of cash in local record shops, just stockpiling as much new metal as he could lay his hands on, but, strangely enough, doesn't remember Ulrich ever mentioning any ambition to form a band of his own.

Nevertheless, the seeds had been planted. When Ulrich returned to the States after the Diamond Head tour, he capitalized on his childhood hobby of bashing pots and pans—and later a small drum kit his grandmother bought for him—by placing an advert for like-minded musicians in an LA rag.

Sean Harris of Diamond Head, Metallica's biggest influence.

The genesis of Metallica

The Gods of Thunder must have looked down and smiled. One of the first replies Ulrich received was from an 18-year-old metalhead called James Hetfield, a man who enjoyed getting his ears bent by Black Sabbath and Venom, a man who modestly claimed he could play guitar and sing "a bit". In fact, Hetfield had been playing guitar since his early teens, following two years of classical piano tuition. He'd already begun playing out his rock-star fantasies in high school bands like the dodgily monikered Leather Charm when he replied to Ulrich's ad.

Hetfield and Ulrich had in fact met before the fateful ad appeared, enduring some unsuccessful rehearsals that Hetfield eventually ended because, as Ulrich would later admit, his drumming back then was "crap"!

Metal Massacre

However, by the time of the second Hetfield/Ulrich union, Ulrich had

Diamond Head was the biggest band of the NWOBHM—but they missed out on long-term success.

badgered Brian Slagel—a mover on the LA scene and boss of the fledgling Metal Blade label—into accepting a track for a compilation LP he was preparing, *Metal Massacre*. There was but one hitch when Ulrich landed his first record deal. He had no band, or song! What he had, though, was a juicy incentive for Hetfield to join forces with him and break out of the going-nowhere, high-school band scenario.

Hetfield acquired another guitarist, Lloyd Grant, for the great recording session on a dismal little four-track machine, and the "band" were away—or so they thought. Penning a track called 'Hit The Lights'—which owed more than a little to Diamond Head's 'Shoot Out The Lights'—as recording commenced, Ulrich and James decided that Lloyd Grant wasn't cutting it as a lead player and quickly recruited another local axeman, Dave Mustaine, to add some solos to the lumpy slice of garage metal they'd lovingly concocted.

The X factor

Slagel was more impressed by the results than he'd thought he'd be. 'Hit

The Lights' had a spark to it which signalled that, even at this embryonic stage, the Ulrich/Hetfield alliance had the all-important X factor. *Metal Massacre* was duly unleashed, with the band's first-ever public mention being incorrectly spelt as "Mettallica" on the sleeve. Grant's credit, and that of newly recruited bass player Ron McGovney, were also misspelt. The band were partly to blame. They'd settled on the name Metallica at the last minute, after working their way through the entirely inappropriate Red Vette and the slightly more palatable Blitzer.

Metal Massacre—which also featured contributions from Steeler, Malice and Ratt—did well, selling over 10,000 copies, but by the time it had been devoured by the US underground metal scene Lloyd Grant had departed Metallica with little more for his trouble than a good story to tell his grandchildren.

Hit the lights

The band quickly made a demo, which featured 'Hit The Lights', plus two cover versions, Savage's 'Let It Loose' and Sweet Savage's 'Killing

Dave Mustaine— talented, fiery and not long for Metallica!

Time'. Ireland's Sweet Savage at the time boasted another star of the future, guitarist Viv Campbell, who cut his teeth with Dio before joining Whitesnake and later Def Leppard. The tape was strong enough to get

Opposite: James Hetfield, already cranking out those mighty riffs!

**Biff Byford of Saxon,
Brit metal warriors
supported by
Metallica in LA.**

the band shows in the LA clubs—most profitably one supporting Saxon at the Whiskey A-Go-Go, a booking that made it considerably easier for the band to find more gigs.

However, Metallica really began to forge the reputation that lifted them out of the pack when they stepped in as last-minute headliners at the Roxy after Swiss numbskulls Krokus had pulled out of the show at the last minute. Metallica performed a rasping and brutal set that brought the house down.

James Hetfield came into his own as a frontman during 1982, with a stage presence that's still unmistakable today.

19

The much-loved bassist Cliff Burton pictured in his much-loved Misfits T-shirt. He quickly formed a solid partnership with Ulrich.

The pivotal demo

Rolling up their sleeves, the band began to write more and more material, until they had enough for what was to become their pivotal demo, *No Life Til Leather*, a seven song-strong tape that is undoubtedly one of the first true thrash metal recordings. The tracks the band recorded were 'Hit The Lights', 'Seek And Destroy' (still in the band's set today, and something of a classic track), 'Motorbreath', 'Phantom Lord', 'Metal Militia', 'Jump In The Fire' and 'Mechanix'.

Metallica's extreme speed was unparalleled—certainly as far as US audiences who'd never witnessed British band Venom were concerned. The time was right for the band to make their first forays up the Pacific coast to San Francisco, where a Bay Area metal scene was already making a racket.

Bay Area 'Bangers

Metallica's almost immediate acceptance into the San Francisco metal scene was both a boost for the band and yet a catalyst for inevitable change. A network of bands and fans that was known affectionately as the Bay Area 'Bangers had the underground metal scene buzzing, with attention focused on the regular Monday night shows at the Old Waldorf club.

Metallica quickly built a following in San Francisco—mainly on the back of the amazing speed and ferocity of their shows, which was generated by a growing on-stage rivalry between Mustaine and Hetfield. Mustaine, as he's since demonstrated at the helm of Megadeth, just loves that spotlight!

Meanwhile Hetfield, though no wallflower, was thinking more deeply about the band than merely finding better ways of upstaging the flame-haired axeman. For a while, he seriously considered handing over vocals to a regular frontman so that he could concentrate on the chugging, monstrous, whiplash rhythm guitar that was becoming the heart and soul of the youthful and yet already potent Metallica sound. Hetfield's suggestion for a frontman was John Bush, then of new metal pacesetters Armoured Saint, now fronting thrash stars Anthrax.

Dave Mustaine (second left) lines up with Megadeth, his post-Metallica outfit.

Cliff Burton arrives

A more pressing problem, though, was that of Ron McGovney. The feeling within the band was that McGovney was adding nothing to their sound. He had to go. They found McGovney's ready-made replacement in San Francisco. Cliff Burton was a tall, geeky, laconic metalhead twanging the four string for a very minor league Bay Area outfit called Trauma. Although it took Burton a while to disentangle himself from Trauma, he was in the band by the time everyone celebrated the brand new year of 1983 with high hopes for Metallica.

Ulrich, to the fore as ever, decided to approach Brian Slagel to finance an album, an offer Slagel had to refuse on account of his own tight budgets. However, the NWOBHM underground was to rescue Metallica just as frustration threatened to snuff out their ambition.

Johnny Z

Johnny Zazula was another metal freak in the Ulrich mould. He was as wide as Ulrich was thin, and equally garrulous. He and his wife Marsha ran a record store in a New York market that specialized in NWOBHM material and demos from hot new US outfits. *No Life Til Leather* found its way there, and both Zazula and Marsha immediately recognized its potential. Zazula, a sharp entrepreneur, decided at that point that Metallica were the band for him. When Ulrich called, Zazula, who had begun operating under his professional moniker of Johnny Z, immediately offered Metallica enough money to relocate to New Jersey for some East Coast shows.

Kirk Hammett. Metallica had kept an eye on his progress with Exodus...

23

Z bought a shit-hot band soon to be accompanied by a shitload of trouble. The Dave Mustaine situation was becoming out of hand. Mustaine was a sleek player, fast and smooth, but his temperament, fuelled by a reputedly high intake of drink and drugs, was as fiery as his red hair. The band delivered the news after one of their first New York shows, and Mustaine immediately packed his bags and headed back West to begin his own band.

Mustaine exits the Metallica story here, but his talent was not so easily denied. He built Megadeth around his inventive riffing and sneering, sarcastic vocal delivery. They now boast worldwide success and a string of multi-platinum albums.

Fretboard whizzkid

Metallica had been keeping an eye on Mustaine's replacement for several months. He played with a Bay Area band who had supported Metallica at one of their Old Waldorf shows. The band was Exodus and the guitarist they were about to lose was a diminutive fretboard whizzkid called Kirk Hammett.

Hammett was already in possession of a wicked technique, courtesy of his guitar teacher, Joe Satriani, an incredibly dextrous musician who would find significant solo success of his own. Satriani also counted David Lee Roth and Whitesnake guitarist Steve Vai as former pupils.

Although he was entrenched up to his neck in the blasting Bay Area scene, Hammett had roots in the first explosion of San Francisco music, getting his early kicks checking out Jimi Hendrix and the Grateful Dead. Metallica whisked the boy to New York and straight into rehearsals for their début album, which Z was determined to fund.

Z and Marsha put their money where their mouths were for Metallica, plunging themselves into debt in order to provide the $10,000 (£6700) plus that Metallica clocked up in their six weeks at America Recording Studios in Rochester, New York State—and when the A&R men's reception of the finished product was no more than lukewarm, Z decided to set up his own label, Megaforce. From such desperation sprang the roots of one of the largest-grossing

rock bands in the world today, and one of the most influential independent labels of the age. Z tied up all-important distribution deals for Megaforce, with Relativity in the US and Music For Nations in the UK. The distribution deal was crucial to the album's eventual success, and laid down roots that proved a great springboard for the band.

Metallica's line-up firmed up. Left to right: Cliff, Kirk, Lars and James.

Kirk Hammett cut his teeth on *Kill 'Em All*.

Kill 'Em All

Ulrich came up with a suitably gross concept for the LP title and artwork. The title was *Metal Up Yer Ass*, and the artwork featured an arm holding a machete coming out of a toilet bowl! Backing off from that idea for reasons of taste and the possibility of discouraging distributors, Ulrich then coined the title *Kill 'Em All*, which soon stuck.

The album featured six tracks from *No Life Til Leather*, plus a reworking of the seventh tune, 'Mechanix', now retitled 'The Four Horsemen'. Tagged on to those were some newies, most notably the lightning-fast 'Whiplash', inspired by the band's headbanging fans, and a grindfest titled 'Anesthesia (Pulling Teeth)'. The album featured a slightly more tasteful cover design—a sledgehammer covered in fresh blood!

Kill 'Em All immediately sold respectably to the band's burgeoning US fanbase, thus relieving the Zazulas' immediate financial problems. In the UK, results were equally encouraging. Although the NWOBHM was blowing itself out, Iron Maiden, Def Leppard and Saxon were among those who survived the fall-out and were building big careers. Metallica jumped on the back of heavy metal's fresh new blood and won a rapturous reception from the underground.

Seven Dates of Hell

A tour was now well in order, and Z backed Metallica with his second signing to Megaforce, a UK band called Raven, who, although not taken too seriously in their homeland, were finding greater success in the US. Metallica played some 38 dates on that first US tour, which culminated in a frenzied return to San Francisco, where the band were met with a heroes' welcome.

The scene was thus set for the band's first European shows. Their name had gone before them, thanks to the intricate tape-trading network in operation throughout the UK and Europe, and now they were before their eager public, albeit supporting Newcastle thrashers Venom on their semi-legendary, semi-comical Seven Dates of Hell tour.

The tour actually consisted of six European shows, climaxing at the

Cliff Burton in typical follicle-challenging action!

Aardschock Festival in Holland. The "Festival" was, in fact, an indoor gig where Metallica shredded heads on a bill that also featured Venom and Tokyo Blade.

After their Aardschock triumph Metallica found themselves at a crossroads—a situation they were fast becoming used to. As with many young hopefuls, there was talent in the band and belief surrounding it, but no money. Metallica played a music that seemed impossibly brutal and uncultured to those in the mainstream music industry. Quivering A&R men would hardly put their jobs on the line for a bunch of young, gawky kids who got their kicks from speed and didn't speak the record company language.

Music For Nations

Z was anxious for the band to record the follow-up to *Kill 'Em All*, but could not finance the project alone. Music For Nations, massively impressed by the Aardschock show and the reception afforded to *Kill 'Em All*, agreed to finance a second album in return for the option on a third.

Metallica had their lifeline, and its importance to them cannot be over-estimated. Had the band had to wait even six months, or maybe a year, for finances to appear, their momentum might well have vanished. As it was, Metallica could keep the hot streak burning.

Metallica say cheese... Well, James does!

CHAPTER TWO

Out of the Thrash Pack

Metallica, kicking off 1984 in the studio to record *Ride The Lightning*.

Metallica entered the studio in February 1984 to begin work on the *Ride The Lightning* album. Ulrich must have felt at home; the venue was Copenhagen. The choice of producer illustrated the vast contortions that heavy metal was undergoing. Flemming Rasmussen came to Metallica fresh from his work with trad rockers Rainbow and their *Bent Out Of Shape* set.

Although work on the backing tracks for the album went well, two old and by now familiar ghosts returned to haunt the band. Internally, James Hetfield was again giving serious consideration to abandoning his role as vocalist and reverting to rhythm guitar. This time, the band made a serious approach to Armoured Saint warbler John Bush, who turned the band down flat. As no one else could come up with a better candidate, Hetfield remained.

Externally, Johnny Z remained under great financial pressure. He had lost money to his US distributors, and Metallica had invested most

of their income on the European tour with Venom. And when recording work on *Ride The Lightning* finally wrapped, Metallica had quite effortlessly bust their original budget by a considerable amount.

Live in the UK

Frustration was building. Metallica felt, rightly, that they had a killer album in the can, but they had still not played live in the UK, and had played a mere five shows in Europe. The band travelled from Copenhagen to London when they believed they were to play a UK tour with two other Megaforce/Music For Nations bands, the Rods—led by ex-Rainbow and Black Sabbath singer Ronnie James Dio's cousin Dave "Rock"

While the Rods didn't make it, they can boast about having had Metallica support them!

Cliff (left) and James give the English fans a taste of what they're missing...

Fienstein—and Exciter. However, the British public's love affair with Metallica was yet to blossom. Ticket sales for the tour were alarmingly awful, and it was cancelled immediately. Desperate to get Metallica in front of a UK audience, Z and Music For Nations hurriedly arranged a gig at

London's legendary fleapit the Marquee, a tiny black sweatbox of a venue situated on Wardour Street, in the heart of Soho, the West End's red light district.

Metallica's UK début finally went ahead on March 27 and was quickly followed by another show at the same venue two weeks later, which was swelled by a number of fans turning up on the word of mouth underground buzz the band's frenzied début had whipped up. Cliff Burton in particular was an instant hit. Committing fashion suicide in his Misfits T-shirt and bell-bottom jeans, headbanging wildly and grinning like crazy, he broke down the usual fan/musician barrier. It was appropriate. Thrash was coming straight to the streets from the streets and there were, as yet, no rock stars involved.

The band's return to Europe was plotted to fill the gap between the second London show and the planned July release of *Ride The Lightning*. They hooked up with Twisted Sister on an unlikely double bill. Sister were as theatrical as Metallica were street. Led by Dee Snider, a gigantic, loud-mouthed, cross-dressed New Yorker, Twisted Sister played hard-edged bubble-gum metal that was seemingly at

Twisted Sister, making up an unlikely double bill with Metallica.

33

Metallica, shifting rapidly through the gears on *Ride The Lightning*.

odds with Metallica's neck-stretching speed. Their attitudes, though, were the same, and Metallica returned to London filled with optimism.

Ride The Lightning
Ride The Lightning was released in late July, and it was immediately obvious that Metallica had shifted rapidly through the gears since *Kill 'Em All*. Although 'Creeping Death' and 'Fight Fire With Fire' ripped through like an out-of-control Grand Prix car, an epic instrumental 'Call Of Ktulu', 'For Whom The Bell Tolls' and 'Escape' proved that the band's outlook, and skills, were on a steep learning curve.

The feeling within the band was that they had broken through a big barrier into uncharted ground. History has proved their point. *Ride The Lightning* is a seminal thrash classic, standing with fellow Bay Area blasters Exodus's brutal *Bonded By Blood* and Los Angeleans Slayer's wicked and visceral *Reign In Blood* as the albums that pretty much defined the genre.

Metallica had proved that a thrash band needn't necessarily have to play fast to provide insane heaviness and by the time the band returned to America at the end of the summer of 1984, *Ride The Lightning* had sold 85,000 copies in the UK and Europe. Megaforce were holding up their end of the bargain Stateside, too. Without a tour to support it, *Ride* had almost repeated its European sales in the US.

A change of management

Lars Ulrich, already beginning to assume his role of band spokesperson and business leader, was the first of the four in Metallica to realize that they could not expect too much more success while they remained with independent management and labels. If Metallica wanted to play with the big boys, a major record deal and heavyweight management

James (left) and Kirk slam it to New York...

were required. Johnny Z had put everything on the line for Metallica, but he was astute enough to realize that the band were probably right. However, that didn't stop relationships between him and the band deteriorating rapidly.

When Metallica played at the Roseland in New York City there were many big hitters present, getting their first look at the underground phenomenon that was now too big for its tiny roots. Among those at the Roseland show was Q-Prime, a dynamic and rapidly expanding management group fronted by Cliff Burnstein and the abrasive Peter Mensch.

Mensch was rapidly acquiring a legendary reputation for his abrupt manner and ruthless business acumen. Q-Prime soon had the band a major deal with the Elektra label for the US. Johnny Z, though, was not totally forgotten. He struck deals that ensured he deservedly shared in Metallica's

James Hetfield, letting it all hang out!

future success. Elektra immediately re-promoted *Ride* in the US, while Metallica returned to Europe for more shows that took them right through to Christmas of 1984.

Meantime, in the UK, Music For Nations released the brain-rattling 'Creeping Death' as an EP. The EP's B side, though, had the greater significance. Metallica covered Diamond Head's classic 'Am I Evil?' and Blitzkrieg's 'Blitzkrieg'.

It was the first time they had acknowledged on vinyl their debt to the NWOBHM, and it marked the way for the *Garage Days Revisited* EP that would mark their resurrection from later catastrophe.

Monsters Of Rock

The band kicked off the new year back home in the US, where they teamed up with Armoured Saint for a tour, thus enabling John Bush to get an eyeful of just exactly what he'd turned down! The tour was an enormous success and the two bands developed a high level of respect for each other—as well as developing a nightly competition to blow each other off stage!

When W.A.S.P. joined the tour the alcohol consumption stakes were raised yet again, and Metallica were soon glorying in the nickname Alcoholica (they were soon to enjoy a legendary photo shoot where they posed with a giant bottle of vodka superimposed with an Alcoholica logo, which, reportedly, didn't go down well with Peter Mensch!). Metallica broke off the US tour for

Kirk Hammett blowing Armoured Saint off stage!

James Hetfield slaying 'em at Donington in 1985.

their biggest gig to date, an appearance at the Donington Monsters Of Rock festival, the UK's largest outdoor metal event, held at the Donington Park raceway in the Midlands. It could have been disastrous. Donington '85 lined Metallica up with ZZ Top, Marillion, Bon Jovi, Ratt and Magnum—a potentially catastrophic mismatch.

Metallica, though, just went on and slayed 'em. The contrast of the bill showed the band up for what they were—an uncompromising, primal force, devoid of star pretension. Metallica were growing up.

Another big festival followed, at San Francisco's Day On The Green, where they were teamed with Ratt again, and also the Scorpions and Y&T. Metallica were rising out of the thrash pack; the seeds of their eventual mainstream acceptance were being sown. The band could appeal to straightahead rock fans as well as to disciples of the extreme.

James and Kirk firing on all cylinders.

James Hetfield settling down with the frontman's role.

Master Of Puppets

By the end of 1985, Metallica found themselves booked back into Copenhagen's inappropriately titled Sweet Silence studios to record a follow-up to *Ride The Lightning*, once again with Flemming Rasmussen. The band were now really on the verge of the big time, and this LP would be the first that Q-Prime and Elektra could really get their teeth into.

With finance no longer a problem thanks to the depths of Elektra's pockets, Metallica could hone the eight songs that would become *Master Of Puppets* to a greater degree than ever before. They were chipping away at the last vestiges of the garage that clung to them in favour of a more mature approach that in no way cramped their savagery, as tracks like 'Battery' and 'Welcome Home (Sanitarium)' would prove.

Master Of Puppets was released in March 1986 and marked the band's last album with Music For Nations. Their deal, struck when Z and Metallica were struggling for cash to make *Ride*, was over once the new LP went on sale, and, predictably, it was not to be renewed. Metallica were soon signed to the

Kirk Hammett— setting standards in metal guitar.

41

Ozzy Osbourne, at the peak of his notoriety!

Phonogram label in the UK for a figure in the region of £750,000 ($1,125,000). The signing was no real surprise, as Phonogram were also home to Def Leppard, another of Q-Prime's clients, which gave Mensch and Co some added leverage with the company.

Of course, the ending of their final independent deal meant that Metallica had severed their last links with the street. They were big business. Ulrich's dream of major representation and big bucks record deals were in place. Metallica were ready to be superstars.

Master Of Puppets rapidly started shifting more units than Metallica had ever sold before. It went gold in the UK, with sales of over 100,000 copies, and reached Top 30 in the US *Billboard* Top 200. Q-Prime immediately flexed their muscle and landed the band a US support slot with Ozzy Osbourne. Metallica could not have wanted for more. Osbourne was right at the peak of his notoriety in the US, and he was packing arenas with his mock-horror carnival and outraging crowds wherever he went. From Osbourne's point of view, having the coolest and most extreme street band around was just fine for his credibility.

fractured a wrist skateboarding and ended up at the mic, while Metal Church guitarist John Marshall stepped in to handle rhythm as Hetfield recovered. .

The benefits of having the backing to get on a tour like Ozzy's was to provide immediate results. During the summer of 1986, *Master Of Puppets* sold over half a million copies in the US.

Tragedy strikes

With the US still reeling, Metallica hit the UK in a well-hard double bill with Anthrax. The fans and the media went wild, seeing the bands as the instant antidote to the likes of Bon Jovi, Mötley Crüe and Quiet Riot, who up to now had been dominant in the market.

The tour climaxed at Hammersmith Odeon, followed by a raucous party back at the band's hotel. Metallica were really taking off. They were the hottest new band in heavy metal, and the celebration was richly deserved. In retrospect, it was made poignant by the tragedy that awaited as soon as the band split the UK for another European tour.

Hetfield whipped through America like an out-of-control freight engine!

The tour whipped through the States like an out-of-control freight engine, with Metallica preceding every Osbourne extravaganza with an hour of hate and frenzy. The only black spot occurred when Hetfield

Metallica on stage in 1987, already a major live attraction.

The band played three shows in Sweden, and on September 27, 1986, they journeyed from Stockholm to Copenhagen in Denmark for the fourth show of the tour. Just after they reached Denmark, the tour bus skidded and rammed into a ditch. Cliff Burton was hurled through a window, and was killed as the tour bus landed on top of him in the ditch. The rest of the band suffered only minor injuries. The bus driver was arrested by police as a matter of routine, but was released without charge. Cliff Burton was just 24 years old.

The hole in the band left by Burton's death initially looked as if it would never be filled. He was part of a unit, an arm of a singular force that was wrenched away. As the tributes to him flooded the music press, Metallica faced the decision as to whether to carry on or split. After Burton's funeral, which took place in San Francisco, they decided to carry on; it was, they decided, exactly what Cliff, the ultimate headbanger, would have wanted them to do.

The decision was a relief to Q-Prime, who were already planning a

Jason Newsted had
the hardest of tasks
replacing Cliff.

Opposite: Hetfield
breaking Jason in
gently!

future without Burton. Q-Prime had
overcome tragedies before; Def Leppard drummer Rick Allen lost an arm
in a car crash and triumphed over his
injury, and AC/DC had lost singer
Bon Scott, only to come back with a
new man, Brian Johnson, and their
biggest album to date, *Back In Black*.

Newkid

By the autumn, Metallica had found
their man. After reportedly audition-
ing Megadeth bassist Dave Ellefson,
they settled on Jason Newsted,
who'd been firing the four strings for
a promising Arizona-based thrash
outfit, Flotsam And Jetsam.

By coincidence, Brian Slagel re-enters the Metallica story here. He had picked up on Flotsam's early promise and given them a slot on another of his *Metal Massacre* compilations before offering the band a full album deal. Their début release, *Doomsday For The Deceiver*, was well received, and the band were beginning to make headway when chief songwriter Newsted heard about the Metallica job and decided that it was for him.

Q-Prime booked the band into their first-ever Far East shows in November of 1986, and it was there that Newsted (who had quickly been christened "Newkid") would take his first bow with Metallica. Japan was a relatively easy début for Newsted, for audiences there had no first-hand experience of Burton's loon pants and headbanging! The real test was to come when Metallica undertook a brief US tour, with Armoured Saint back in tow. The band were well-received. Although Burton was obviously very much missed, Newsted was proving a fine acquisition—a hard, fast and accurate player who powered along with Ulrich to give

Metallica an awesome engine, albeit with a less clownish heart.

By the time Metallica returned to Europe, Newsted's induction was almost complete. He came through an emotional show in Copenhagen— the city that the band had been travelling to at the time of Burton's tragic death—before stamping his authority on some familiar Metallica territory, a headline slot at the Aardschock festival in Holland.

With all of the live work left high and dry by Burton's demise now covered, the band returned to San Francisco to begin work on a new LP. However, James Hetfield once again contrived to break an arm skateboarding, thus putting the whole schedule on hold!

Garage days

Recording was shelved for even longer when Q-Prime fielded an offer for Metallica to join headliners Bon Jovi and Deep Purple on the travelling Monsters Of Rock bill throughout Europe. The only snag to a lucrative and appealing offer was that Metallica had nothing to plug. With Lars Ulrich anxious to try out the small

Jason (left) and James. Metallica fulfilled outstanding commitments left by Cliff's death, and Jason handled his task with dignity.

recording unit newly installed in his garage, the idea for an EP of cover versions of tunes that had heavily influenced the band was born. The band recorded six tracks: Diamond Head's 'Helpless', Budgie's 'Crash Course In Brain Surgery', Killing Joke's 'The Wait', Holocaust's 'The Small Hours' and two tunes by the Misfits (Cliff Burton's favourite band), 'Green Hell' and 'The Last Caress'. Christened *The $5.98 EP—Garage Days Revisited*, the EP was pounced on by an eager public. With the record leaping off the shelves, Metallica hit the UK in readiness for their second appearance at the Monsters Of Rock's principal event, the show at Donington Park.

Metallica had leapt to third on the bill, coming on after Cinderella, W.A.S.P. and Anthrax, and before Dio and Bon Jovi. However, the day proved a great disappointment. Metallica, along with W.A.S.P. and Anthrax, failed to spark on a miserable English summer's day. Once they were a safe distance away in Europe, Ulrich wasted little time in announcing that he felt their performance had been "shit"!

CHAPTER THREE

Megaforce Music

Back in the US for the start of 1988, Metallica turned their attention to the new studio album. The original producer was Mike Clink, the hottest name on the scene following his triumph on Guns N' Roses multi-platinum, universe-shattering début album *Appetite For Destruction*. However, a few weeks into recording, Clink was mysteriously dropped in favour of the returning Flemming Rasmussen.

There was a feeling within the band that only Rasmussen could capture the Metallica spirit, and by the end of March, the band had the nine tracks that would make up *...And Justice For All* safely down on tape. The album featured the last remnants of material that Cliff Burton had had a hand in—a nice tribute, and one

that was to be expanded upon by the release of *Cliff 'Em All*, a video release that featured much of the band's private footage of their three years with Cliff Burton. The video is almost a bootleg affair—at that point, Metallica had made no promo clips—and its overriding aim was to show Cliff and the band as they really were, warts and all. Much of the live footage was knockabout stuff, although Ulrich did admit that the last song, 'Orion' was an emotional moment—it was the music they'd chosen for Cliff's funeral. However, true to the man's spirit, there was plenty of fun stuff—which included some clips of Cliff indulging in his beloved weed!

The release did, though, slow down Jason Newsted's process of

Metallica begin the long wait for a producer for ...*And Justice For All.*

51

assimilation into the ranks. He was probably the band member most anxious for ...*And Justice* to be released, as it would establish him as a fully-fledged Metalli-man. However, the launch of an American Monsters Of Rock touring festival, to be headlined by Van Halen, and also featuring Scorpions, Kingdom Come and Dokken, proved too good an offer for Metallica to turn down, delaying the album still further. However, the tour failed to set the public alight, although Metallica were generally perceived to have emerged with the most credit.

Once the shows were complete, attention turned back to ...*And Justice For All*, now being remixed by the Steve Thompson/Mike Barbiero team who'd hit the heights with Guns N' Roses' *Appetite for Destruction*. The album was completed in August

Opposite: Metallica in 1988. From the left: Kirk, Lars, James and Jason.

Right: **Jason Newsted's initiation into Metallica was completed by ...*And Justice For All*.**

Kirk Hammett, a redeeming factor on ...And Justice.

the material was mostly beyond dispute—the likes of 'One', 'Blackened' and the awesome 'Harvester Of Sorrow' stood up to anything the band had done before. However, the controversial introduction of acoustic guitars on the less intense 'To Live Is To Die' caused some backbiting, as did the frankly dreadful production and mix. The album sounded dry and

and finally released on September 8. In the two and a half years since the release of *Master Of Puppets* Metallica had expanded fast, and expectations were at fever pitch. While *...And Justice* flew out of the box like a bat out of hell, seasoned Metallica watchers were preparing a semi-deserved backlash. The quality of

James Hetfield, Metallica's driving force.

rasping, with drums pushed up as loud as Ulrich's personality, and poor Newsted's basslines virtually obliterated! Only Hetfield's convincing roar and the way his guitar meshed with Hammet's salvaged the record.

The tone of *...And Justice For All*, though, was unmistakable. Metallica had shifted permanently away from their breakneck speed roots and, via lengthier workouts like the LP's title track, were expanding their horizons into the mainstream. Some nitpicking was to be expected—it goes with the territory. But Metallica had effectively broken with a very channelled past. Now, anything was possible.

A creative triumph

Having concocted a stage set that featured a collapsing Statue of Liberty as its centrepiece, Metallica began the Damaged Justice tour in Edinburgh, Scotland, on September 24, 1988. As Europe and then America fell to them, Metallica—or was it Q-Prime?—decided that the extra kick into superstardom could be achieved by the band's first promo clip, a film for the single 'One'. It was perhaps surprising that the band agreed to have the track edited down from its seven and a half minutes of pounding horror to a more palatable four minutes. The accompanying clip, though, was a creative triumph.

The song had been inspired by Dalton Trumbo's novel *Johnny's Got His Gun*, the story of a Vietnam veteran who lost both arms and both legs in the war. Footage of the subsequent film of *Johnny's Got His Gun* was intercut with some menacing black-and-white shots of Hetfield crooning and then screaming the lyric. 'One' turned into a graphic clip

James Hetfield produced his most convincing vocals to date on 'One'.

that powered the single into the US Top 40 and the UK Top 20. The track gained Metallica a nomination for a Grammy Award. The whole thing ended in shambles, though, with the award for Best Heavy Metal Song going to the ageing British folk-rock combo Jethro Tull!

That aside, Metallica had now taken on epic proportions. The US had fallen to them, as had Europe and the Far East. The tour just grew and grew. Metallica had been used to playing theatres holding 2000–4000 people, but they were now effortlessly ensconced on the "Shed Circuit", pulling in between 10,000 and 15,000 people a night. They performed relentlessly for 18 months, never turning down a gig. The tour eventually ground to a halt at the end of 1989, after 251 gigs. There could be no doubt that with ...And Justice Metallica had ascended to rock 'n' roll royalty. Even the Grammys made amends early in 1990, when 'One' was belatedly honoured.

After resting through the new year of 1990, Metallica lined up a brief UK and European jaunt in May, an event that Q-Prime ensured would not be

Lars (left) and Kirk. Awards? We got 'em!

without a product to promote when Phonogram released *The Good, The Bad And The Live*, a boxed set of all of Metallica's EPs plus some previously unavailable live material.

Going for world domination

Obligations fulfilled, Metallica spent the summer and early autumn sketching material for another studio LP. The shit really hit the fan, though, when their choice of producer was announced. Bob Rock was famous —maybe infamous—for his work as a soft rock, commercial knobsman who'd produced Mötley Crüe, Aerosmith, and, most horrifically of all as far as Metallica rivetheads were concerned, Bon Jovi!

Ulrich was quick to defend their choice, claiming that Rock had a feel for Metallica's particularly vicious groove. In a series of interviews given once the LP and tour were eventually released, Ulrich gave numerous mentions to a meeting that the band had had with Q-Prime when work on the album was under way. They had decided that Metallica would make every supreme, gut-busting effort to make the album and tour as huge, as commercially massive as they possibly could. No interview would be turned down, no venue unplayed. Metallica were going to attempt world domination, and the new album was a good start.

Rock simplified the band's sound from the inglorious melée that infested ...*And Justice For All*. Riffs were still as heavy as reinforced concrete, but smoothed out into a palatable roar. 'Enter Sandman' was an obvious single, with its radio-friendly, growl-along-with-James chorus, while 'Nothing Else Matters' and 'The Unforgiven' were almost balladic in execution. The band had, if it's possible, cut a mainstream extreme

Metallica won a much-deserved Grammy Award—the music business's equivalent of an Oscar—in 1990 for the single 'One'.

James Hetfield, now one of rock's best-known frontmen.

metal album! Where they were once brutal and simplistic, Metallica were now epic; where they were once a brief two fingers to the establishment, they were now its prodigal, big bucks-earning son. But whatever the criticism, the spirit and heart of the band were still present on the album, which is officially untitled, but known simply as *Metallica*.

The album sleeve, though, provoked much hilarity. It's an all-black affair, relieved only by a just-visible black snake curled in one corner. The inevitable comparisons to the spoof metal band Spinal Tap's semi-legendary *Smell The Glove* cover were produced loudly and often, with Ulrich almost visibly exploding whenever he was quizzed about it!

Straight to the top

With the release of the album butting up against the long-awaited second and third Guns N' Roses LPs (*Use Your Illusion I* and *II*), a battle royal was forecast, with perhaps only Metallica and Q-Prime convinced that they could outstrip the biggest rock 'n' roll band on the planet.

To kick off the *Metallica* tour (dubbed "Wherever I May Roam" after one of the LP tracks), the band made their biennial appearance at the Donington Monsters Of Rock festival, this time as the second-on-the-bill attraction to veteran boogie kings AC/DC—another big kick for super-fan Ulrich. The Monsters bill progressed at a stately rate through Europe and climaxed at Moscow's

Lars (left) and James prepare to do battle with Guns N' Roses over the summer of 1992!

James Hetfield astride the Metallica "snakepit" stage—a rock god in action!

Tushino airfield, where the band played to a crowd estimated at over 500,000 people.

Metallica emerged while the band were in Europe, and, to their astonishment, entered the US *Billboard* Top 200 at Number 1. When the band returned to America, it was to a

James in traditional pose—and riffing hard!

heroes' welcome. Metallica had constructed a unique, diamond-shaped stage that enabled them to play "in the round", and also enabled 120 very lucky fans to watch the show from a specially constructed "snake-pit" contained within the stage. After criss-crossing the US, Metallica flew to London to appear at the Freddie Mercury Benefit show at Wembley Stadium, where they joined the world's élite for the tribute to the late Queen star—another major coup for a band used to being outsiders.

Outstripping Guns N' Roses

The summer of 1992 was the summer that America was almost crushed under the weight of the heaviest tour since the Civil War! Metallica teamed up with Guns N' Roses for a stadium-dominating extravaganza from which Metallica gained all of the credibility and Guns N' Roses drew the dingbats, following Axl Rose's incitement of a riot in Montreal. Hetfield was particularly scathing about Rose in interviews he gave after the tour's completion.

The strategy of exposing the "Black Album" in every way possible

was an unbelievable success. The LP has sold six million copies in the US, and another five million world-wide. The band toured everywhere from the Pacific Rim to Britain and back again—over 300 shows that took them into the summer of 1993.

With a live album and a video planned for release at the end of 1993, Metallica's domination is complete. There is talk of a year off, but already Ulrich is getting itchy feet. And remember what happened the first time the crazy Dane got moving...

James on stage with Jim Martin of Faith No More during the summer of 1992.

63

CHAPTER FOUR

Band Profiles

Lars Ulrich

Lars Ulrich is undoubtedly the most famous drummer in heavy metal, and probably the most high-profile drummer in the music business. It was his massive enthusiasm for heavy metal that created Metallica, and much of their success is down to his incredible work rate. Ulrich is heavily involved in the business side of the band, just loves to give interviews and also delights in the ligging and attendant socializing that being in the world's biggest heavy metal band engenders. His high profile works against him in the press, who often mistake enthusiasm for ego. However, within the band Ulrich enjoys the total respect of the other members, and he'll defend them to the hilt in return.

"No matter how much he pisses you off, you know he's working hard for the band," says Jason Newsted.

Lars Ulrich—he drums and poses for photos, too!

"You may be sitting in the plane waiting for him for three-quarters of an hour, but you know that's 'cos he's making sure that something happens next week. We really do rely on each other. If one of us is weak, then we're all weak.

"He says every day that everyone has a role in this band. His role is partly as a go-between for band and management and industry, holding stuff together, making sure stuff happens in order to get the band in the right place."

Ulrich's heart and soul is in Metallica. There is a revealing scene in the band's fly-on-the-wall documentary of the making of the *Metallica* album where Ulrich and Hetfield are at each other's throats, a confrontation that ends with the former smashing his drumstick through the skin of the drum. The point they were arguing seemed small, but not to Ulrich. His devotion to the perfecting of Metallica is unswerving.

Tennis to rock

Ulrich has never lost sight of what it feels like to be a fan, because, at heart, he still is one. He just happens to be in a bigger band than many of his heroes! Even as the Wherever I May Roam tour kicked in with shows as a part of the travelling European Monsters Of Rock bill, he was deeply thrilled to be appearing with Antipodean boogie legends AC/DC. Similar appearances throughout the world with the likes of Iron Maiden and Deep Purple had the same effect. And Metallica's monumental US tour with Guns N' Roses in the summer of 1992 was driven on by Ulrich's enthusiasm for Guns and the power of the double bill they could construct together.

James Hetfield was often scornful of Ulrich's obvious enjoyment of hanging out and partying on that tour, but Lars didn't care. He's still living out his dreams, and loving every minute of it.

Those dreams began when he discovered heavy rock music via his father's record collection, and saw Deep Purple in concert in his native Denmark at the tender age of nine. He was hooked on metal from that moment on, and his other planned career as a tennis player began to take a downward path.

Lars, an enthusiastic partygoer both on and off stage.

It was tennis, though, that took Ulrich from Denmark to Florida to study at a tennis academy. And study he did—but mainly at the local metal record store, which had begun to stock products by the rapidly growing legions of hungry young UK bands lumped together under the NWOBHM masthead. Ulrich threw himself into the music with unwavering devotion. Diamond Head in particular blew his mind, and he flew to England in 1981 to follow one of their tours and to immerse himself fully in the scene.

It was no passing fad. Ten years after the NWOBHM's glory days of 1982, Ulrich took time out to put together a multi-band compilation, *The NWOBHM Revisited*, along with journalist Geoff Barton, whose work in the now-defunct weekly UK rock paper *Sounds* had kept Ulrich posted

Lars Ulrich in thudding action, Metallica's driving force.

> "No matter how much he pisses you off, you know he's working hard for the band. We really do rely on each other. If one of us is weak, then we're all weak."
> **Jason Newsted**

> **"Everyone has a role in this band. His [Lars's] role is partly as a go-between, making sure stuff happens in order to get the band in the right place."**
> **Jason Newsted**

that brought him into contact with James Hetfield. Hetfield was a step ahead of him musically at that point. In fact, the pair had already met for rehearsals once before and Hetfield had pulled out because he felt that

Lars's importance for Metallica extends far beyond his drumming.

while he was in the States. And when Diamond Head re-formed for a long-overdue second bite of the cherry in 1993, Ulrich was immediately on hand to get the band press attention, advise on their comeback LP *Death And Progress* and generally get the vibe up and running.

Drumming for success
Ulrich has made massive strides as a drummer since he began Metallica with that fateful LA newspaper ad

Right and opposite:
**Lars Ulrich whips
up the Metallicrowd
—it was Lars who
initiated many of the
band's big breaks.**

Ulrich hadn't yet developed the necessary technical skills.

With typical tenacity, though, Ulrich stuck with it. On the *Metal Massacre* LP track 'Hit The Lights' and on the *No Life Til Leather* demo he began to show promise, on *Kill 'Em All* he was a highly proficient speedster, and by *Master Of Puppets* he was capable of propping up

70

numbers as varied as 'Master Of Puppets', 'Battery' and 'Orion'. Jason Newsted's rapid development as an excellent bass player also upped the stakes for Ulrich, and anyone who caught the Wherever I May Roam tour can vouch that Metallica would not be the ferocious and lean unit they are without Ulrich's engine room.

It was Ulrich, too, who possessed the foresight and ambition to whip Metallica's career along after a promising start with Johnny Z's Megaforce and the UK's Music For Nations. While others may—and indeed have—been willing simply to settle for what they have and stagnate as a result, Ulrich would not. The story goes that he contacted Peter Mensch from a phonebox and grasped the management deal that gave Metallica all the clout they needed for a big future.

Lars Ulrich's contribution to Metallica goes far beyond his drumming. No band could ask for a more enthusiastic or attentive musician. Though much maligned, he has in fact enabled Metallica to become what they are today—the biggest band in heavy metal.

James Hetfield

Right and opposite: James Hetfield in action—not bad for a guy who didn't want to be a singer!

For a guy who didn't want to be a singer, James Hetfield has made a decent fist of fronting Metallica to worldwide glory. Hetfield wears his angst and fury on the outside when he's on stage—a big, tall man with ratty blond locks and a Fu Manchu beard, clad all in black, legs splayed apart, right arm chopping down at his guitar, eyes open wide, lyrics spat from a curling lip. Off stage, a more laconic persona takes over; Hetfield enjoys shooting pool with his mates, listening to country and western

music and hunting. The trappings of stardom so beloved by Lars Ulrich are laughed at by Hetfield.

Ulrich and Hetfield are Metallica's fulcrum, and yet two more different characters you couldn't wish to meet. Their relationship is a complex one, but it's absolutely essential to Metallica's future well-being. And yet, from the Guns N' Roses leg of the Wherever I May Roam tour, there were rumours that they were having disagreements. Indeed, Hetfield quite

"James may get angry with Lars with the time he takes on the drums, but if you looked him in the eye and asked him who his best friend is, he'd say Lars."
Jason Newsted

frequently told the press that he disapproved of the backstage ligging and socializing that Ulrich threw himself into.

However, as with most close friendships, theirs is never as it may seem to the outsider. Commenting on the pair's relationship, bassist Jason Newsted said: "They dig at each other all the time and talk shit, but they're best friends. James may get angry with Lars with the time he takes on the drums, but if you looked him straight in the eye and asked him who his best friend is, he'd say Lars. Sometimes they need this angst. It's creative tension. If it was all nice and sweet all the time, it wouldn't work. Things are much deeper-seated than that."

The creative tension has worked to great effect for Metallica. Each of the albums is generated when Ulrich and Hetfield begin to sift through the ideas and riffs that are floating around, and then start work on arrangements. Although guitarist Kirk Hammett's contributions are vital and Jason Newsted is slowly beginning to have more of his songs and ideas accepted, Ulrich and Hetfield pull the whole thing together. As the pair who kicked Metallica off in the first place, they surely have the greatest understanding of its dark core.

A musical upbringing

Just 18 years old when he first met Lars Ulrich, Hetfield had been raised in the Christian Scientist faith but was possessed of a rebellious streak that still runs through him. He had been interested in music from an early age, and had trained for two years in classical piano before he was given the traditional rock 'n' roll start—a cheap guitar bought by his mum! He got into Black Sabbath and Van Halen, and had his first taste of the rock 'n' roll live experience at one of AC/DC's LA shows.

Hetfield fooled around with high-school bands, playing all the usual covers, but soon found that writing his own material was far more satisfying. He was already looking for the step ahead when he met Lars Ulrich and had the carrot of a track on the *Metal Massacre* album dangled under his nose.

Metallica's early compositions were speedy imitations of their NWOBHM heroes, but even on the *No Life Til Leather* tape the seeds of greatness were already apparent. 'Metal Militia' was a neat speedblur, while in 'Seek And Destroy', Metallica had penned a song so popular that they still retain it in their live set, with entire stadiums wailing along to its whiplash chorus. *Kill 'Em*

Opposite and above: Two typical studies in aggression...

James gets physical with the fans. From humble beginnings, he's now metal's best-known frontman.

All, although naïve, was packed with a promise that flowered a mere year later on *Ride The Lightning*. By the time of *Master Of Puppets*, Hetfield's compositions were immense and intricate, though always memorable, and he's still stretching himself today. On the *Metallica* album 'Nothing Else Matters' was a courageous departure, with the world's most renowned one-time thrashers employing an orchestra to get the song's rich textures across properly.

Fierce and fiery

Hetfield's fierce independence has made him the centre of several controversies. When Axl Rose wanted to bring Ice-T on to the Guns N' Roses/Metallica double bill, Hetfield baulked at the prospect and was accused of racism. It was a charge

he refuted with typical forthrightness, claiming that the fact that he didn't like rap music didn't make him a racist. Was a black man who didn't like country and western music racist?

He was outspoken in his opinions of Guns N' Roses'—and in particular frontman Axl Rose's—behaviour on the tour, an argument that stemmed from a show in Montreal where Hetfield suffered quite severe burns to his arm in a pyrotechnics accident on stage. With Metallica having to cut their set short, he expected Guns N' Roses to fill the breach. Instead, Rose quit the stage early and a riot consequently ensued.

He was accused of jingoism when 'Don't Tread On Me' emerged in the wake of the Gulf War (though the songs had been written back in 1990, before the fighting began), and has also received flak for his love of hunting, which he celebrated in the song 'Of Wolf And Man' from the *Metallica* set.

Hetfield admits he likes to keep himself to himself when he's away

James Hetfield:
"Metallica is our
lives, but it's not
the only thing we
enjoy doing."

"As you grow older, you tend to respect what each person wants to do with their life. Metallica is our lives, but it's not the only thing we enjoy doing."
James Hetfield

from the touring environment. "I've never really liked people much, anyway," he confessed to UK magazine *Kerrang!* "As you grow older, you don't really grow apart from each other, but you tend to respect what each person wants to do with their life. Metallica is our lives, but it's not the only thing we enjoy doing."

James Hetfield sounds like a man who's sussed out just what he wants from life, and, to the relief of all his fans, Metallica still looms large in it.

Kirk Hammett in live action. Not flash, not fussy, just a great, cool player.

Kirk Hammett

Kirk Hammett does not fit the criteria of the traditional axe hero. Slight of build, with a baby face surrounded by black locks and a wispy beard, he doesn't really resemble a Slash or a Keith Richards. Nope, Hammett has the job for all the right reasons: the grinding riffs, ripping licks and shredding solos he pulls off night after night on tour, and across Metallica's greatest recorded moments.

While Hetfield and Ulrich are embraced by the media as the figureheads of the band, Kirk Hammett and Jason Newsted quietly get on with the job of making Metallica the giant, bellowing beast that it is. While Hammett is no limelight hogger, pick up any muso mag with a poll for top guitarist in it and you'll always see his name near as dammit at the top of the list. His secret is a simple one. He never overplays, unlike so many of the other much-admired lead players. You'll find Hammett taking each song, each riff, each solo on its own merits; he'll plug the space with just the right amount of flash fingerburn or ear-endangering heaviness.

Kirk Hammett, transcending humble beginnings.

Kirk Hammett was born on November 18, 1962 in the Mission district of San Francisco, one of the less desirable parts of the city. He attended school with Primus's main man Les Claypool. Hammett was into music from a very young age, being just old enough to catch the back end of the hippy explosion for which San Francisco was so famous in the late Sixties. Hendrix, Santana and the Grateful Dead were early influences, along with the prerequisite band Led Zeppelin.

Hammett began his six-string education at the age of 15, pulling in his hippy influences along with those of Aerosmith and Thin Lizzy, plus the burgeoning new metal scene, and the illiterate fury of punk rock. His first band was a garage outfit called Mesh, and he fooled around with several others before getting serious with Bay Area blasters Exodus.

Exodus had quickly won a reputation on the Bay Area scene, at around the same time that Metallica were first making their mark. (In fact, Hammett supported his future bandmates at one of the Old Waldorf gigs.) Although Exodus were not developing at the same pace as Metallica, the same passion and fury was present in their music, and they would later cut a seminal thrash classic called *Bonded By Blood*, which ranks right up there with the likes of *Ride The Lightning* and Slayer's gruesome *Reign In Blood.*

Hammett was unaware that the band he supported at the Waldorf were having serious problems with their talented axeman Dave Mustaine. For their part, Metallica had already spotted Hammett's potential,

and were quick to summon him from San Francisco to the East Coast just as soon as Mustaine had received his marching orders. Obviously aware of Metallica's huge potential and burgeoning reputation, Hammett did not take too long to jump the Exodus ship and join up.

Six-string star

Metallica had gained a guitarist with an immaculate technique, and a

Kirk was taught guitar by Jo Satriani. Now the pupil is a master!

"**The worst thing that can be said about me has already been said; that I'm a total shit, crap guitar player. And you know what? On certain nights I have to agree! Hey, we're only human!**"
Kirk Hammett

Kirk's primary consideration is the song.

great appreciation of many different styles of playing. The major part of Hammett's formal tuition came from Joe Satriani, a remarkably dextrous musician whose outrageous ideas and playing were beginning to revolutionize the modern guitar sound. But while many of the young guitarists influenced by the likes of Satriani, Steve Vai and Swedish virtuoso Yngwie Malmsteen merely used songs as a vehicle for displaying their flashy manoeuvres, Hammett was instinctively different; the song is

his primary consideration, and he's a far better musician for it.

Metallica were also fortunate that Hammett had worked out some of his desire for rock 'n' roll excess before he was incorporated into the band. "When I first joined the business, I got it all out of my system then," he told UK's *Raw* magazine. "I also went through a really bad drug period, and I'm glad it happened before rather than after I got a lot of success. If I'd had the money to experiment with drugs, I'd have been a wreck. Now, I'm just not bothered."

As Metallica ascended to superstar status, Hammett was able to follow the example of one of his guitar heroes and move out of the deprived background he came from. Telling *Raw* about his proudest moments, he commented: "[I played] with Carlos Santana at the Bammies [Bay Area Music awards]. To be trading off with him on stage was musically spiritual. We've travelled along similar lines. We're both from the Mission district of San Francisco, we both play guitar. He's been around for 20 years, though, and we've been around for 10. But moving back to

San Francisco into a big house...it took me 30 years to get out of the ghetto, but I made it. Hope that doesn't sound too cornball."

Hammett's role in the band is certainly an unsung one, compared to the life bathed in limelight. It doesn't bother him. "You have to listen to the people that say that [you're crap] as much as the people who say you're great. The worst thing that can be said about me has already been said; that I'm a total shit, crap guitar player. And you know what? On certain nights I have to agree! Hey, we're only human!"

Kirk in action: "A great appreciation of many different styles of playing."

Jason Newsted, a quiet character with a cool look who faced the toughest job in rock 'n' roll—filling Cliff Burton's boots.

Jason Newsted

When Jason Newsted was recruited to replace the late Cliff Burton as Metallica's four-stringer, he faced the most thankless task in rock 'n' roll—filling the boots of a dead hero. Cliff was not only a great player, he was granted special status by fans who loved his grin that ran as wide as the stage he was standing on, his mad flares, his wild headbanging.

Newsted is a quieter character with a cooler look. The best thing he

> "When I got into the band, I had to be tested. Those guys had been through so much together. They couldn't have someone in the band who weakened them."
>
> **Jason Newsted**

ever did was not try to be Cliff Burton. By now Newsted has been Metallica's bass player for longer than Burton was, and his acceptance, he feels, is complete.

"It's taken five or six years for my songwriting to be accepted, to get them to listen," he admitted during the Wherever I May Roam tour. "At first my biggest part was playing live, but that's okay, because my strength

Jason's main strength is his superlative live playing.

When Newsted joined Metallica he walked into a very emotionally charged situation. The band rehearsed him and then went straight out on the road, first to Japan and then back to America, for a tour that included a show in Burton's hometown of San Francisco. There was no chance for Newsted to establish himself by appearing on a new album before he was in front of Metallica's public.

Indeed, the covers EP *Garage Days Revisited* aside, Newsted had been in Metallica for a month short of two years when *...And Justice For All* was issued. It was a tough induction, a time that required strength of character to work through.

Now Newsted is an integral part of the Metallica sound. As he says, the live arena was where he first made his mark, quickly forging a hard-driving rhythm partnership with Lars Ulrich. It was on musical terms that Newsted could first establish his credentials as a worthy replacement for Burton. Metallica had been on a steep learning curve since the naïve days of *Kill 'Em All*. Newsted was able to steady the ship and allow the

is in the live show. With my songwriting, I was trying to puncture the shell that these guys put up; the way they protect their art and hold it dear.

"It strengthened all of us. It took that long for the mutual respect to grow. When I got into the band, I had to be tested. Those guys had been through so much together. They couldn't have someone in the band who weakened them."

"I'm still a big Metallica fan. I've gotta say that Metallica are the hardest-working, most dedicated and determined band around. As an outsider I thought so, and now I'm an insider, I think the same thing"
Jason Newsted

Jason gives James some vocal back-up. He's "an integral part of the Metallica sound".

band the freedom of a rock-solid base on which to refine their sound. He's a neat, tight player, with an unfussy style that comes with an appreciation of the great blues players and the spaces in their music that they created.

Hooked by Kiss
When Newsted first heard about the Metallica job he was playing with Flotsam And Jetsam, a Phoenix-based trash band who had made a decent start with an album called *Doomsday For The Deceiver*, a

89

> "I still get nervous and excited about meeting a couple of hundred kids who've waited for us after the show. I still get excited about playing. The standard is very, very high in this band. Each night, I still really enjoy playing those songs."
>
> Jason Newsted

Opposite: Jason Newsted, still a big Metallica fan at heart!

basic, speedy thumper to which Newsted had contributed the majority of the songs. His enthusiasm had also cast him in the role of chief gig-booker, manager and press agent and although Flotsam were beginning to pick up useful press and underground acclaim, Newsted didn't waste any time agonizing over his decision to go for the Metallica job.

As he remembers, "I didn't sleep for a week practising!"

Jason Newsted's background could hardly be less rock 'n' roll. His family owned a ranch in Michigan which specialized in horse-breeding, and his early ambitions lay in that area. However, he underwent the traditional American teenage rock 'n' roll baptism and was totally hooked by his first Kiss album. He began playing bass aged 14, trying his damnedest to be Gene Simmons. He soon caught on to Black Sabbath, though, got into Geezer Butler—a great, wristy, jazzy player—and began expanding his horizons.

When Newsted arrived in Phoenix in 1984, he quickly pulled Flotsam together with vocalist Eric AK. Ironically, considering the start Metallica got off to, Flotsam's first lucky break also came from Brian Slagel's *Metal Massacre* series. They contributed 'I Live You Die' to *Metal Massacre VII*.

In another ironic twist, Flotsam And Jetsam supported Dave Mustaine's Megadeth when they ran through Phoenix on tour. Flotsam have never really recovered from Newsted's departure, although they

are still together and have a major deal with the MCA label.

Honest at heart

"I'm still a big Metallica fan," Newsted admits. "I've gotta say that Metallica are the hardest-working, most dedicated and determined band around. As an outsider I thought so, and now I'm an insider, I think the same thing." When reminded that he too had had to put in the work, Newsted retorted, "Yeah, and I get to reap the rewards!"

Right and opposite:
Jason Newsted: not
a party animal—at
least, not off stage!

Newsted has also retained his initial wonder at the size and scope of the band he joined. He still gets a massive kick out of the adulation Metallica inspire, and that must be a huge help to his bandmates.

"You learn a little bit more about taking things in your stride," he says. "You learn about getting recognized when you go out, and by other performers you've always looked up to. I can't speak for the other three guys, but I still get nervous and excited about meeting a couple of hundred kids who've waited for us after the show. I still get excited about playing. The standard is very, very high in this band. Each night, I still really enjoy playing those songs."

Off stage, Newsted is the antithesis of the rock 'n' roll star. "I'm not a party animal. I'm not a beer drinker. I get my relaxation in other ways. I'm lucky. Music is my occupation and

> **"I'm not a party animal. Music is my occupation and my hobby. I love playing all kinds of music—funky music, blues music. For the past couple of years, my main thing has been researching all those old blues guys."**
> **Jason Newsted**

my hobby. I love playing all kinds of music—funky music, blues music. For the past couple of years, my main thing has been researching all those old blues guys."

It's hard to think of another band that Newsted could be in. At heart, Metallica are an honest and simple band. "Metallica got famous through hard work," he asserts. "We're honest, genuine people."

The Albums

KILL 'EM ALL

**Megaforce (US),
Music For Nations (UK)**
July 1983

Tracks: 'Hit The Lights', 'The Four Horsemen', 'Motorbreath', 'Jump In The Fire', '(Anesthesia) Pulling Teeth , 'Whiplash', 'Phantom Lord', 'No Remorse', 'Seek And Destroy', 'Metal Militia'

Burton (left) and Hetfield: killin' 'em all live on stage!

While *Kill 'Em All* is not a classic début album—it's as simplistic and naïve as its cover, which features a sledgehammer covered in blood—its spitfire riffing and overwhelming wide-eyed self-belief are utterly convincing. Metallica didn't know much when they began recording (after all, their whole studio experience ran to the recording of 'Hit The Lights' for Metal Blade's seminal *Metal Massacre* compilation, and the seven tracks featured on the *No Life Til*

Leather demo), but what they did know was that a decent riff should be gunned out loud and often, and that lack of technique could be overcome by fiery commitment to the cause.

In retrospect, Kill 'Em All is one-track and frenzied, whipping by at breakneck speed but leaving little behind once admiration for its sheer endeavour has waned. If that criticism is harsh, it's because Metallica have set such high standards since.

To assess the full impact of Kill 'Em All, it's necessary to set the album in its time. Metallica were getting off on the sheer energy of the New Wave of British Heavy Metal bands and their Bay Area contemporaries, but they had little else for reference points. Venom aside, no one was approaching the extremes of speed that Metallica were touching. Anthrax's Fistful Of Metal came later in 1983, Exodus's seminal Bonded By Blood was two years away, and Slayer's definitive study of brutality, Reign In Blood, would not arrive until four years hence. By the standards of what was around, Kill 'Em All, while not revolutionary, was certainly ahead of its time.

Metallica re-recorded six of the No Life Til Leather demo tracks for Kill 'Em All, while the seventh track, 'Mechanix', was reworked as 'The Four Horsemen'. Where No Life Til Leather was a typical garage tape, poorly mixed and hopelessly rough, Kill 'Em All was sleek by comparison. In particular, the new versions of

Kirk Hammett, purveyor of whiplash riffs on Kill 'Em All.

Kirk (*right*) and
James (*opposite*),
driving six-stringers
on *Kill 'Em All*.

'Metal Militia' and 'Motorbreath' showed massive gains in pace and accuracy. 'Hit The Lights', though, remains charmingly shabby. The first song that the band ever wrote, it owes a huge debt to the likes of Diamond Head and Holocaust.

Of the new material, 'Pulling Teeth (Anesthesia)' is as painful as it sounds, while 'Seek And Destroy' is the standout track. A madly revving engine with a hugely screamable hookline, it remains a staple of Metallica's live set today—not bad for a ten-year-old thrash tune.

The individual performances on *Kill 'Em All* show that Lars Ulrich still had some catching up to do on the standards set by Hetfield's already recognizable chug, Cliff Burton's head-rattling rhythm and Hammett's dextrous digits.

Metallica broke ground with *Kill 'Em All*, which was lapped up by the underground scene at the time, and were soon to prove that they could extend beyond speed over content. That it's still listenable to ten years on—where much NWOBHM material is not—is further testimony to a strong début.

RIDE THE LIGHTNING

**Megaforce (US),
Music For Nations (UK)**
July 1984

Tracks: 'Fight Fire With Fire',
'Ride The Lightning', 'For
Whom The Bell Tolls', 'Fade
To Black', 'Trapped Under Ice',
'Escape', 'Creeping Death',
'The Call Of Ktulu'

One year on, Metallica were exhibiting a rate of growth more rapid than a plague of locusts; for many people, *Ride The Lightning* is Metallica's finest album and one of the all-time great metal LPs.

From the turbulent opening track 'Fight Fire With Fire', it's immediately apparent that Metallica had zipped through the gears following 12 solid months of gigging and the corresponding maturing of both their sound and songwriting. Where *Kill 'Em All* was built purely for speed, *Ride The Lightning* showed that Metallica's sheer heaviness was just as effectively conveyed via a gigantic brooding riff like 'For Whom The Bell Tolls' or the epic expanse of the instrumental 'Call Of Ktulu' as it was on the speedfreak riffage of 'Trapped Under Ice'.

Metallica's adventurous embracing of new styles led to a mini-backlash among devotees of tunes like 'Metal Militia' and 'Whiplash'. 'Escape', perhaps the least heavy track Metallica have ever cut, added fuel to their fire. However, the majority were quick to embrace *Ride The Lightning* as the far more complete package that it was.

The band were quick to defend *Ride The Lightning*, explaining that their music had to move on. Indeed,

James Hetfield:
exhibiting a rate of
growth faster than a
plague of locusts on
Ride The Lightning.

with Ulrich slowly hatching his master plan—major management, major record deal—it's readily apparent that the band had to prove to themselves and to the outside world that there was substance to them and to their music; that they were a long-term prospect who could learn, album by album, tour by tour, and also that they were a band who could drag their rabid fanbase along with them.

To that end, then, *Ride The Lightning* had to develop the traditional Metallica theme without diverting too far from the sound that had created such a stir for the band. With many others in the burgeoning Bay Area of San Francisco picking up the Metallica/Anthrax vibe, it was again down to the foursome to provide the lead.

Considered in that light, *Ride The Lightning* is a massive achievement. It was recorded just as the band hit the cusp of stardom. That was an important factor insofar as Metallica still possessed the fire in their bellies that fuelled their inception. Thus, although the title track is a sophisticated slab of heavy metal, it's also possessed of an attitude that just

dares you to doubt the passion of Metallica's new direction.

That said, though, *Ride The Lightning*'s most enduringly popular cut is 'Creeping Death', an utterly monstrous maelstrom of speed and hate.

The guitars of Hetfield and Hammett mesh with the rapidly tightening rhythm section of Ulrich and Burton to provide a wild ride that is guaranteed to fill the dance floor of any rock club to this day.

Metallica cut an instant classic in *Ride The Lightning*.

MASTER OF PUPPETS

**Megaforce (US),
Music For Nations (UK)**
February 1986

Tracks: 'Battery', 'Master Of
Puppets', 'The Thing That
Should Not Be', 'Welcome Home
(Sanitarium)', 'Disposable
Heroes', 'Leper Messiah',
'Orion', 'Damage Inc'

MASTER OF PUPPETS

"I don't think
the word thrash
applies to us. We
were the originators
of that style, but
we've always
looked beyond
that."
Lars Ulrich

Master Of Puppets is the album that
completed the journey from the
extremes of thrash to the metal
mainstream. It is sleek and sophisticated, gut-wrenchingly powerful, with
a vicious edge to it, but mainstream
none the less. Ulrich admitted as
much: "I don't think the word thrash
applies to us. We were the originators of that style, but we've always
looked beyond that."

Metallica were now scornful of
bands that engaged in a crazy race
to prove themselves the ultimate
speedfreaks. *Ride The Lightning*
proved that Metallica could be heavy

and slow; *Master Of Puppets* proved that they could be heavy and subtle.

Over 50 minutes in length, *Master Of Puppets* provided everything the metalhead could want in an album. You want face-ripping pace? There's 'Battery'. You want a chug in your chest that feels like a heart attack? There's 'Welcome Home (Sanitarium)'. You want an epic that runs the gamut from slowly menacing acoustic moments to gargantuan, pounding riffage and Hetfield's most ear-blastin' grasp? Then there's 'Master Of Puppets' itself.

Master Of Puppets was the first Metallica album to be free from financial restraints, as Elektra were now funding the band. Thus Ulrich could fuss endlessly about his drum-sound, Hammett was free to overdub to his heart's content, and Hetfield could get to grips with the most convincing vocal performance he had given to date. He manages to appear tortured, sarcastic, hateful and awesome in equal measure.

Flemming Rasmussen was really on top of the Metallica sound, too. At times the band whip up an invincible maelstrom, and yet, amid all the speed-blur, each component in the engine can be heard to be working both as an individual part and an essential piece of the whole.

James blasts it out: *Master Of Puppets* brought the band to stardom.

James Hetfield
grinds out the riffs to
Master Of Puppets.

The line-up for *Master Of Puppets*— Cliff Burton's swansong.

Metallica's deal with Q-Prime also had an effect on their direction. Secure in the knowledge that their medium-term future at least was assured, the band could relax and explore honestly every avenue they felt held promise. So you get an instrumental like 'Orion' slapped up against 'Leper Messiah', one of *Master Of Puppets*' most brutal tracks, and both work to equally good effect.

Master Of Puppets opened the door and showed Metallica their future. With a massive fanbase ready to leap on anything they could come up with, it was apparent that the band could develop and refine, comfortable in the knowledge that they were accepted in their own right and not just as a part of a happening scene like thrash metal.

Master Of Puppets perhaps lacks the balls-out hunger of *Ride The Lightning*, but what's missing there— and it's not very much—is more than compensated for by the breadth of the canvas. Metallica, by the evidence of *Master Of Puppets*, were stars in the making. The album's a landmark in every respect.

...AND JUSTICE FOR ALL

Elektra (US), Vertigo (UK)
September 1988

Tracks: 'Blackened', '...And Justice For All', 'Eye Of The Beholder', 'One', 'The Shortest Straw', 'Harvester Of Sorrow', 'The Frayed Ends Of Sanity', 'To Live Is To Die', 'Dyer's Eve'

...And Justice For All is ultimately a disappointment. With their star status sealed, Metallica lost a little focus. They wrote some fantastic songs—the quality of 'One', 'Blackened' and 'Harvester Of Sorrow' can hardly be disputed—but the delivery was sloppy and the production was not far short of disastrous.

On the Damaged Justice tour that followed the album's release, the Metallica stageshow was capped by a rickety model of statue of Justice that collapsed into pieces at the climax of the shows. *...And Justice For All* is as lopsided and precarious as that statue.

Problems began when the band first recruited Guns N' Roses hotshot

...And Justice For All **was Metallica's ticket to superstardom—but ultimately the album is a disappointment.**

Metallica—out past their bedtimes!

Mike Clink to handle the production, but then parted company with him in favour of Flemming Rasmussen once the backing tracks were laid down. According to Ulrich, that had always been Metallica's plan. If so, it was a strange one. If it was a case of hanging on for 12 weeks for Rasmussen to be available—as was claimed—then why not just wait? After all, Metallica were not under pressure to get the job done.

So ...And Justice For All had an off-kilter start and never really recovered. The finished product is bizarrely mixed. Ulrich's drums are as upfront as his personality, while the guitars that provide Metallica's usual chug are dry as sandpaper, and lacking in any real substance.

As it was the first album since Cliff Burton's untimely demise (although the band had recorded and released the *Garage Days Revisited* EP), Jason Newsted was especially anxious for it to emerge and establish him as a fully-fledged member of the band, especially as the *Cliff 'Em All* tribute video was still fresh on the counters. He must have been sorely disappointed—his bass is as near as dammit buried in the mix.

The reasons for the final sound have never really been discussed at length by the band. Perhaps because ...And Justice For All marked the first time that Metallica had plenty of time and money to decide exactly when and where to record, they dithered and dallied instead of just knocking the LP out as they had done with *Kill 'Em All* and *Ride The Lightning*.

However, a band of Metallica's stature were never going to record a disastrous album, and ...*And Justice For All* is ultimately redeemed by the quality of the songs on offer. Opener 'Blackened' flies out of the traps like a bat out of hell, mad, bad and dangerous to listen to! Hetfield went on record to say that 'Blackened' was a deliberate poke in the eye to all those expecting an LP full of lengthy epics!

'One' is an instant classic. It is the grisly story of a Vietnam veteran trapped in a torso after his arms and legs have been blown off, and Hetfield is utterly convincing in his narration. 'Harvester Of Sorrow' is another of the band's face-removing chuggers that rattle to you like an overladen freight train, while 'Dyer's Eve' is an underrated thumper, too. The title tune, though, is overworked and overlong, and 'The Frayed Ends Of Sanity' is a throwaway.

If ...*And Justice For All* had come unheralded from an unheard-of band, it would have been hailed as a great achievement. But in the light of Metallica's previous two releases, judgement must be a little harsher. Could do better.

Metallica: the biggest heavy metal band in the world—and probably the best!

METALLICA

Elektra (US), Vertigo (UK)
August 1991

Tracks: 'Enter Sandman', 'Sad But True', 'Holier Than Thou', 'The Unforgiven', 'Wherever I May Roam', 'Don't Tread On Me', 'Through The Never', 'Nothing Else Matters', 'Of Wolf And Man', 'The God That Failed', 'My Friend Of Misery', 'The Struggle Within'

Bob Rock! Bob Bloody Rock! That was the world's reaction when it was announced that the producer of such lightweight, radio-friendly critical cannon-fodder like Bon Jovi and Mötley Crüe would handle the next Metallica record. It was like asking Walt Disney to direct a snuff movie!

It's to their overriding credit, then, that Metallica and Rock pulled it off. *Metallica* (as the album is generally known—it's officially untitled, as is

The band took a decision to make *Metallica* as massive as possible.

Led Zeppelin's fourth LP) is smooth but muscular, harsh and heavy-weight without being rasping. The improvement from ...And Justice For All is huge, and this must be due, at least in part, to the 251 dates on the Damaged Justice tour finally cementing Newsted's status and shaping Metallica into a more mature and complete unit.

Orchestras and religion

Hetfield, too, rose to the challenge, producing his finest lyrics, along with another throat-threatening, uncompromising vocal performance. For 'Nothing Else Matters' he produced a lyric about love while being on the road (and ended up using a 40-piece orchestra on the stately recorded version!), and via 'The God That Failed' he tackled the strict religious upbringing in the Christian Scientist faith that had dogged his adolescence. For a man who began by writing about blood, thunder, hellfire and mythical gods, it was a huge and brave departure.

Elsewhere, though, he ran into trouble for the content of 'Don't Tread On Me', a jingoistic, pro-American anthem that emerged at the time of the Gulf War. Hetfield, however, had penned the tune back in 1990, so much of the furore was provoked by the change in world circumstances and some unlucky timing.

But the lead-off track is the tune that really broke Metallica to those who had never been exposed to their music before. 'Enter Sandman', with its hooky riff and shriek-it-out chorus, was an instant classic. In fact, the tune was voted Greatest Metal Song Of All Time above 'Stairway To Heaven' and 'Smoke On The Water' by the readers of UK metal magazine Kerrang!

When Metallica decided to do everything possible to promote the album, they could be safe in the knowledge that they had a mature and vibrant product to back up their hard work. They no longer sound like the super-aggressive young hotheads who cut Ride The Lightning. They're a mature and sophisticated rock band who play by their own rules. Metallica sounds liberated, unconstrained by commercial expectations. It sounds honest. After ten years, you can't say better than that.

James Hetfield, standing alone as frontman for heavy metal's greatest stars—for years to come!

Chronology

1981 Lars Ulrich places an ad in a Los Angeles paper for musicians, and hooks up with James Hetfield. Bassist Ron McGovney and fiery guitarist Dave Mustaine are soon recruited. Their first song, 'Hit The Lights', appears on the *Metal Massacre* compilation.

1982 Metallica begin gigging in LA, quickly attracting a core following.

Summer: They relocate to San Francisco to join the thriving Bay Area Thrash scene, and make rapid inroads there, too.

1983 New York entrepreneur Johnny Z persuades the band to relocate once again. Ron McGovney is replaced by Cliff Burton, ex-Trauma. Mustaine is fired and Exodus axe-slinger Kirk Hammett steps in.

July: *Kill 'Em All*, Metallica's début album, is released.

1984 Metallica undertake their first European tour, supporting Venom. They record their second LP, *Ride The Lightning*, which is released in July. The band grab a management deal with the big-hitting Q-Prime team, and land a major deal with Elektra in the US.

1985 A year of consolidation as Metallica tour hard in Europe and the US. The band's year is capped by an appearance at the legendary Monsters Of Rock festival at Castle Donington in the UK.

Autumn: The band begin work on their landmark third album, to be titled *Master Of Puppets*, with producer Flemming Rasmussen.

1986 *Master Of Puppets* is released in February. During a triumphant European tour, Cliff Burton dies in a tour bus crash in Denmark.

Summer: The band recruit former Flotsam And Jetsam bassist Jason Newsted. They complete their US and European schedules.

1987 Metallica record and release the *Garage Days Revisited* EP. In August, they make their second appearance at the Donington Monsters Of Rock festival, before hunting for a studio and producer for their forthcoming LP.

1988 After a brief dalliance with Mike Clink, Flemming Rasmussen produces *...And Justice For All*, the band's first LP for their new UK Label, Phonogram. It is released in September 1988.

1989 **April:** 'One' is released as a single, accompanied by the band's first ever promo video. Metallica launch into a massive world tour that sees them ascend to superstar status.

1990 Winding up the massive, 251-date tour, the band take a break for almost the first time ever. They announce the surprise choice of producer for their next LP, Bob Rock.

1991 **August:** The long-awaited album, simply titled *Metallica*, is released to worldwide acclaim. The band begin a monumental tour in support.

1992 Metallica hook up with Guns N' Roses for the tour of the year. Rumours of a feud between the bands follow a riot at a show in Montreal!

1993 The Wherever I May Roam tour wraps up in the summer. Metallica are unchallenged as the world's biggest metal band. The tour was seen by more than 4 million people, and worldwide LP sales stand at over 20 million!

Discography

ALBUMS

Kill 'Em All
July 1983
US: Megaforce MR 1069
UK: Polygram 838142-2
Highest chart position: US –, UK –

Ride The Lightning
July 1984
US: Elektra 60396-2
UK: Vertigo 838140-2
Highest chart position: US –, UK 87

Master Of Puppets
February 1986
US: Elektra 60439-2
UK: Polygram 838141-2
Highest chart position: US 29, UK 4

...And Justice For All
September 1988
US: Elektra 60812-2
UK: Polygram 836062-2
Highest chart position: US 6, UK 4

Metallica
August 1991
US: Elektra 61113-2
UK: Vertigo 510022-2
Highest chart position: US 1, UK 1

SINGLES

'Jump In The Fire'
January 1984
US: Not released
UK: Music For Nations PKUT 105
Highest chart position: US –, UK –

'Creeping Death'
November 1984
US: Not released
UK: Music For Nations 12KUT112
Highest chart position: US –, UK –

'Harvester Of Sorrow'
September 1988
US: Not released
UK: Vertigo METAL 212
Highest chart position: US –, UK 20

'One'
April 1989
US: Unavailable; UK: Vertigo METAL 5
Highest chart position: US 35, UK 13

'Enter Sandman'
August 1991
US: Unavailable; UK: Vertigo METAL 7
Highest chart position: US 16, UK 5

'The Unforgiven'
November 1991
US: Unavailable; UK: Vertigo METAL 8
Highest chart position: US 35, UK 15

'Nothing Else Matters'
April 1992
US: Unavailable
UK: Vertigo METAL 10
Highest chart position: US 34, UK 6

'Wherever I May Roam'
June 1992
UK: Unavailable; UK: Vertigo METAL 9
Highest chart position: US 82, UK 25

'Sad But True'
September 1992
US: Unavailable; UK: Not released
Highest chart position: US 98, UK –

COMPILATIONS

***The Good The Bad And The Live:
The Six-And-A-Half Year 12-inch Collection***
Contains all of the band's EPs and singles up till
and including 'One', plus three new live tracks,
'Harvester Of Sorrow', 'One' and 'Breadfan'
May 1991
US: Unavailable
UK: Vertigo 875487-2
Highest chart position: US –, UK –

The $5.98 EP—Garage Days Revisited
'Helpless', 'The Small Hours', 'The Wait',
'Crash Course In Brain Surgery',
'Last Caress/Green Hell'
August 1987
US: Elektra 9607757-4
UK: Vertigo METAL112
Highest chart position: US 28, UK 27

VIDEOS

Cliff 'Em All
1987

***A Year And A Half In The Life Of Metallica
Parts I and II***
1992

Index

Picture Acknowledgements

Photographs reproduced by kind permission of **London Features International**; **Redferns**/M. Cameron, /Fin Costello, /Peter Cronin, /Mick Hutson, /Ebet Roberts; **Retna**/Jay Blakesberg, /Chris Chinn, /Steve Double, /Van Iperen, /Johansson, /B. Kuhmstedt, /Micelotta, /Tim Mosenfelder, /Tony Mottram, /Neal Preston, /Scott Weiner, /T. White; **Syndicated International Network**.
Front cover picture: Retna Pictures.